Aural Time!

Practice Tests for the New Revised ABRSM Syllabus and Other Exams

Grade 7

DAVID TURNBULL

CONTENTS

Published by
Bosworth & Co. Limited
14–15 Berners Street,
London W1T 3LJ, UK.

Exclusive Distributors:
Music Sales Limited
Distribution Centre, Newmarket Road,
Bury St Edmunds, Suffolk IP33 3YB, UK.
Music Sales Pty Limited
20 Resolution Drive, Caringbah,
NSW 2229, Australia.

This book © Copyright 2010 Bosworth.
International Copyright Secured.

Printed in the EU.

Your Guarantee of Quality
As publishers, we strive to produce every book to the
highest commercial standards.
This book has been carefully designed to minimise awkward
page turns and to make playing from it a real pleasure.
Particular care has been given to specifying acid–free, neutral–sized
paper made from pulps which have not been elemental chlorine bleached.
This pulp is from farmed sustainable forests and was
produced with special regard for the environment.
Throughout, the printing and binding have been planned to ensure
a sturdy, attractive publication which should give years of enjoyment.
If your copy fails to meet our high standards,
please inform us and we will gladly replace it.

www.musicsales.com

BOSWORTH
part of The Music Sales Group

INTRODUCTION

Having had the privilege of working with the late David Turnbull on a number of his projects, including the original publication of some of the *Aural Time!* volumes, it is a great pleasure to contribute to this new edition of his work, which takes account of various mainly small revisions to the aural tests of the Associated Board of the Royal Schools of Music examinations, effective from January 2011 onwards.

At Grade 7 the following changes have been made, all of which are reflected in this book:

- In Tests A and B, the part to be sung by candidates is now limited to a range of an octave and the keys used will be restricted to those with key signatures of no more than three sharps or flats in Test A and four sharps or flats in Test B.

- In Test C (ii), candidates will no longer have to recognise the second inversion of the tonic chord: the only chords to be identified will be I, IV, V, V7 and VI, all in root position.

- In Test D (i), questions will be limited to two features of the music (excluding rhythm, although candidates will still have to clap a rhythm from the piece in part (ii) of the test). In questions on the character of the music, candidates will be expected to identify specific musical features of the piece to support their views.

As teachers, many of us have had pupils who are excellent performers but whose examination marks have been let down by weakness in the supporting tests, such as aural. It is important to emphasise to such students that skills such as memory recall (Test A), the ability to internally conceptualise sounds represented by notation (Test B) and analytical listening coupled with a clear understanding of musical terminology (Tests C and D) are not hurdles designed to make examinations harder but are essential tools for musicians in many different branches of the art.

The first two aural tests for Grade 7 require a sung response (although it is worth remembering that candidates can opt to play instead of sing in Test A). As in the earlier grades, those who worry about singing should be reassured that tone doesn't matter – they can hum or whistle if they prefer – it is only pitch and rhythm that are assessed. The part to be sung will lie within a range of an octave and candidates may tell the examiner the range within which they prefer to sing if they wish.

The questions in Test D at Grade 7 are broadly similar to those encountered at Grade 6, but pupils should be encouraged to provide more detail in their answers whenever possible, not least because this will provide excellent advance preparation for the student-led discussion required in Test D at Grade 8. Study of the commentaries at the end of this book will show the type of responses that could be made although these are not, of course, the only possible answers. In particular, teachers should check that pupils know how to justify their views on the character (and, if required, the style and period) of the music played in Test D by referring to specific musical features of the piece. Again, the commentaries at the end of the book will show some of the ways in which this can be done.

Paul Terry
London, 2010

Uniform with this volume: *Aural Time!* Grades 1–6 and 8.

Also by David Turnbull: *Theory Time!* Step-by-step instruction in musical theory and rudiments. Grades 1–5.

All published by Bosworth & Co.

Test A. Singing or Playing from Memory

Pupils must sing or play from memory the lower part of a two-part phrase. The key-chord and the starting note will be played and named, and two bars of the pulse will be tapped. In an examination, the example will be played twice. When giving practice, however, teachers should not hesitate to play the test more frequently, and if necessary be prepared to divide the test into sections. Tests should be played at the keyboard using both hands, so that the separate lines are as clearly defined as possible. *If the example starts with a single part or a unison, the pupil must be warned.*

4

Molto moderato   Vaughan Williams

20

CD Track 15

Lebhaft   Schumann

21

Allegro   Prokofiev

22

CD Track 16

Allegro   Purcell

23

Allegro   Corelli

24

Andante   Bartók

25

CD Track 17

Andante   Bach

26

CD Track 27

CD Track 28

CD Track 29

CD Track 30

CD Track 31

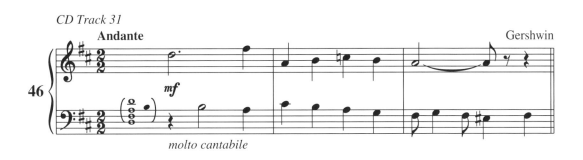

Test B. Sight-Singing

Pupils should be able to sing a short melody, accompanied by a lower part played on the piano. The test may be in any major or minor key up to four sharps or flats. The key chord and starting note will be given, and the pulse indicated.

Andante Linley

27

Molto moderato Vaughan Williams

28

Poco andante

29

Sweelinck

CD Track 53

Allegro Mozart

30

CD Track 54

Lento Old German Lullaby

31

Test C. Cadence, Cadence Chords and Modulations.

Test C1. For Grade 7, pupils must be able to recognise **interrupted** cadences in major and minor keys, as well as the **perfect** and **imperfect** cadences set in Grade 6. *In addition —*

Test C2. Pupils must be able to name the two chords which form the cadence (marked by * in the examples). These chords will be limited to the tonic, subdominant, dominant, dominant seventh and submediant (all in root position).

Chords may be described by their full name (for example,"tonic", "dominant" etc.) or by their number (for example, "I", "V" etc.) or by their letter name (for example, "C minor", "G major" et.c). *In addition —*

Test C3. Pupils must be able to recognise the modulations described on page 20.

Interrupted cadences in Grade 7 tests will consist of the submediant chord (VI) preceded by *either* the dominant chord (V) *or* the dominant seventh chord (V^7).

Perfect cadences in Grade 7 tests will consist of the tonic chord (I) preceded by *either* the dominant chord (V) *or* the dominant seventh chord (V^7).

Imperfect cadences in Grade 7 tests will consist of the dominant chord (V) preceded by the tonic chord (I) *or* the subdominant chord (IV). In practice, IV–V is less frequently used by composers than I–V.

Pupils should be reminded that:

- at the beginning of any test, the keychord will be played. The pupil must memorise the sound of this tonic chord, and decide if the chord is major minor.

- in minor keys, the dominant chord at cadences is major, because of the sharpened seventh.

- in major keys, the submediant chord is minor, but in minor keys the submediant chord is major.

  It follows from the above that —

  (i) if a phrase in a major key ends with a minor chord, the cadence must be interrupted;

  (ii) if a phrase in a minor key ends with a minor chord, the cadence must be perfect.

- the dominant seventh is often used as the first chord in perfect and interrupted cadences, and so pupils must recognise quickly whether the chord concerned is a simple dominant or a dominant seventh.

Some preparatory work on the points above should be done before the following examples are attempted.

Play an example chosen from one of the groups twice, having sounded the keychord first with its tonic doubled in the bass. Ask the pupil to name the cadence. Then play the keychord again, followed by the first of the two cadence chords. Ask its name. Then sound the second cadence chord and ask its name.

Interrupted Cadences

Perfect Cadences

CD Track 63

CD Track 65

CD Track 70

CD Track 68

Imperfect Cadences

CD Track 69

CD Track 64

Test C3 Modulations. Pupils must be able to recognise if a phrase starting in a major key has modulated to the key of its dominant major, to its subdominant major, or to its relative minor.

● Modulations to the dominant major involve a sharpening, and this produces an effect which can be described as "brightening".

● Modulations to the subdominant major involve a flattening, and this produces an effect which can be described as "darkening".

● If a Grade 7 example ends in a minor key, it has modulated to the relative minor.

It may be helpful for pupils to practise these preliminary exercises:

1 Major to dominant major

2 Major to subdominant major

3 Major to relative minor

Test C3 Modulations. The original key chord will be sounded, and then the test will be played once only.

Tonic major to Subdominant

Tonic major to Relative minor

from *A Petits Pas*, 25 Études mignonnes, Leduc
Reproduced by permission of Éditions Heugel et Cie., Paris /
United Music Publishers Ltd.

Tonic major to Dominant

Test D. Questions about pieces.

In Test D of ABRSM examinations the questions on pieces are in two parts.

D (i) Pupils should be able to answer questions about two of the following musical features heard in a piece: dynamics, articulation, tempo, tonality, character, style and period, texture, structure. For practice purposes, a selection of questions is provided for each of the examples that follow.

Before playing the music, tell the pupil which two features the questions will be about (e.g. 'Listen to this short piece, then I'll ask you about its texture and tonality').

When identifying the character, or the style and period of the piece, pupils should try to take account of a range of features heard in the music, rather than relying on just one element.

Comments on the questions about pieces in this section are printed on Pages 37–38.

D (ii) Pupils must clap the rhythm of a short extract from the same piece, and describe it as being in two, three, four or six-eight time. In examinations, candidates will only be asked to clap one example, but to provide more practice two examples for clapping are given for each of the pieces below.

The questions in this section are useful preparation for many other types of music examination, such as GCSE and A-level. Pupils for other examinations can practise writing down *answers instead of giving them verbally.*

CD Track 84

D (i) Questions

(a) **Tonality**: Describe the tonality of this music. Are there any modulations?
(b) **Structure**: Compare the two main phrases in this piece.
(c) **Texture**: Comment on the texture of the *accompaniment* to the melody.
(d) **Tempo**: Does the tempo alter during the piece, or does it stay the same throughout?
(e) **Style and period**: What can you say about the style and period of this piece?

D (ii) Clap one of the following extracts, and say if it is in two, three, four or six-eight time.

CD Track 85

D (i) Questions

(a) **Structure**: Describe the phrase structure of this piece.

(b) **Tonality**: Comment on the tonality of this piece.

(c) **Texture**: Describe the texture in this piece.

(d) **Articulation**: Briefly comment on the articulation of the music.

(e) **Style and period**: What style of piece is this and in which period was it written?

D (ii) Clap one of the following extracts, and say if it is in two, three, four or six-eight time.

CD Track 86

Allegro, ma non troppo

Schumann

D (i) Questions

(a) **Texture**: Comment on how the texture builds up in the first half of this piece.
(b) **Dynamics**: Describe the use of dynamics in this piece.
(c) **Articulation**: Name *two* different types of articulation used in this piece.
(d) **Tonality**: Briefly comment on the tonality of this piece.
(e) **Structure**: What name is given to this type of musical structure?

D (ii) Clap one of the following extracts, and say if it is in two, three, four or six-eight time.

CD Track 87

Sans hâte, avec un peu de mélancolie

Simone Plé

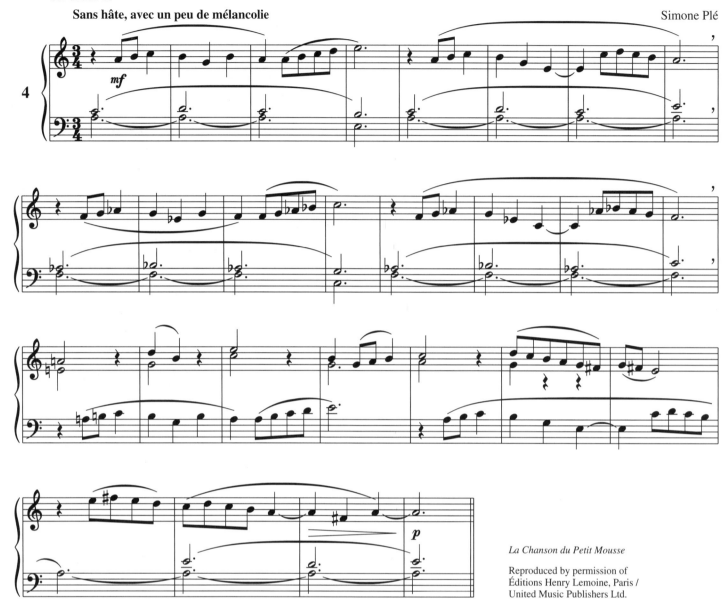

La Chanson du Petit Mousse

D (i) Questions

(a) **Structure**: This piece begins with a phrase that is repeated with a changed ending.
How do the next pair of phrases relate to this opening?

(b) **Texture**: What changes in texture do you notice when the opening melody returns in the second half of the piece?

(c) **Tempo**: Which of the following best describes the tempo of this music?
Allegro   Adagio   Unhurried
Does the tempo change during the piece?

(d) **Tonality**: Is this piece major, minor or modal in tonality?

D (ii) Clap one of the following extracts, and say if it is in two, three, four or six-eight time.

CD Track 88

Tempo di menuetto

Arne *(adapted)*

D (i)   Questions

(a)   **Structure**: How does the melody in the second half of this piece relate to the melody in the first half?

(b)   **Structure**: How are the four phrases in this piece defined?

(c)   **Texture**: Compare the texture of the first half of this piece with the texture in the second half.

(d)   **Tonality**: What can you say about the tonality of this piece?

(e)   **Style and period**: This is a piece from the early classical period. What in the music tells you that?

D (ii)   Clap one of the following extracts, and say if it is in two, three, four or six-eight time.

CD Track 89

D (i) Questions

(a) **Texture**: How does the texture at the very end of the piece differ from the texture at the start?
Can you name one *other* type of texture heard in this piece?

(b) **Tonality**: Is the final cadence major, minor or modal?

(c) **Structure**: In what ways are the three main sections of this piece similar?

(d) **Style and period**: In what period do you think this was written? What in the music tells you that?

D (ii) Clap one of the following extracts, and say if it is in two, three, four or six-eight time.

CD Track 90

Bach

D (i) Questions

(a) **Tonality**: Comment on the tonality of this piece.
(b) **Texture**: Compare the texture in the second half of the piece with the texture of the first half.
(c) **Structure**: Where, and in which part, did you hear a rising scale of nearly two octaves?
(d) **Tempo**: What Italian term best describes the tempo of this piece? Did the tempo change?
(e) **Style and period**: In what period do you think this piece was written?
Which musical features tell you that?

D (ii) Clap one of the following extracts, and say if it is in two, three, four or six-eight time.

CD Track 91

Schönberg

D (i)   Questions

(a)   **Tonality**: Is this piece tonal, atonal or modal?

(b)   **Structure**: What musical feature is used as a unifying device throughout the piece?

(c)   **Articulation**: Comment on the articulation of this music.

(d)   **Tempo**: Describe any changes of speed in the piece.

(e)   **Style and period**: In what period do you think this piece was written?
       Which musical features in the piece are particularly characteristic of that period?

D (ii)   Clap one of the following extracts, and say if it is in two, three, four or six-eight time.

CD Track 92

Andante

Tchaikovsky

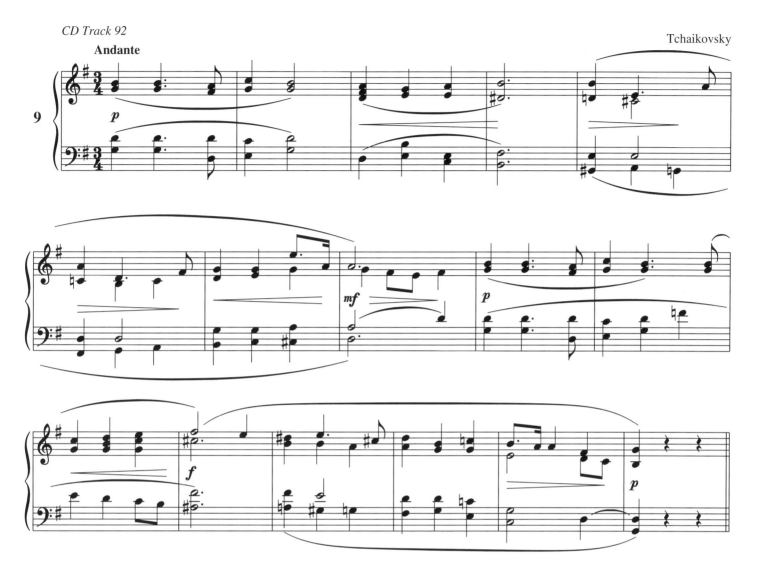

D (i) Questions

(a) **Structure**: There are four main phrases in this piece. In what way are they all similar?

(b) **Texture**: Describe the texture of this music.

(c) **Tonality**: Briefly describe the tonality of this piece.

(d) **Dynamics**: Describe the use of dynamics in this piece.

(e) **Style and period**: In what period do you think this piece was written?
Which musical features tell you that?

D (ii) Clap one of the following extracts, and say if it is in two, three, four or six-eight time.

D (i)   Questions

(a)   **Structure**: What can you say about the phrase structure of this piece?

(b)   **Texture**: Describe the texture of this music.

(c)   **Tonality**: Comment on the tonality of the piece.

(d)   **Character**: What in the music gives this piece its character?

(e)   **Style and period**: What musical features tell you that this is a piece from the classical period?

D (ii)   Clap one of the following extracts, and say if it is in two, three, four or six-eight time.

CD Track 94

[Andante]

Gibbons

D (i) Questions

(a) **Tonality**: Comment on the tonality of this piece, referring particularly to the final chord.
(b) **Texture**: Briefly describe the texture of this music.
(c) **Dynamics**: What do you notice about the dynamics in this piece?
(d) **Style and period**: In what period do you think this piece was written?
      Which features of the music tell you that?

D (ii) Clap one of the following extracts, and say if it is in two, three, four or six-eight time.

[Moderato]

John Blow (*adapted*)

D (i) Questions

(a) **Texture**: Describe the texture of this piece.
(b) **Structure**: What can you say about the structure of the bass part?
(c) **Structure**: What is the musical function of the opening of this piece?
(d) **Dynamics**: Comment on the use of dynamics in this piece.
(e) **Tonality**: Describe the tonality of this music.
(f) **Style and period**: What is the style and period of this piece? What in the music suggests that to you?

D (ii) Clap one of the following extracts, and say if it is in two, three, four or six-eight time.

Appendix. Comments on the questions on music in Test D.

The answers below are not the only possible ones.

No. 1 **(a)** Minor key, no modulations; **(b)** they are identical in length and start the same, but the first (loud) phrase ends on dominant harmony while the second (quieter) phrase returns to the tonic; (c) the accompaniment is thin-textured (two-part) and mostly sustained; (d) it stays the same throughout; (e) the thin texture, simple diatonic harmony, contrasted ('terraced') dynamics and lively rhythm all suggest that this is a baroque dance.

No. 2 **(a)** Ternary (ABA) – A has two main phrases that each start in the same way, and when this section returns the melody is an octave higher; **(b)** major key, with some chromaticism but no modulations; **(c)** melody and accompaniment, with the accompanying chords mainly split into continuous quavers; **(d)** legato, with each pair of short phrases answered by a longer phrase; **(e)** the functional harmony (mainly chords I and V^7) with occasional chromaticism, steady tempo with regular anacrusic phrases in triple metre, repeated rhythms and melody-dominated texture all suggest a dance style (a minuet) from the classical period.

No. 3 **(a)** It starts with a single melodic line (a monophonic texture) which is then imitated by two other parts in succession to create a three-part contrapuntal (polyphonic, imitative or fugal) texture; **(b)** mostly quiet, but a short crescendo near the end leads to a loud final chord; **(c)** mostly staccato, with off-beat accents near the end; **(d)** it starts in a major key (briefly passing to the dominant) and ends in the relative minor; **(e)** fugue (or fugal).

No. 4 **(a)** They are the same, but a (major) third lower; **(b)** the melody is in the bass, and the accompaniment is less sustained; **(c)** unhurried, no; **(d)** modal.

No. 5 **(a)** It is a decorated (ornamented) version of the same melody; **(b)** by imperfect cadences, each followed by a rest in the melody line; **(c)** there is a homophonic texture throughout, but in the first half it is chordal (block chords) while in the second half the harmonies are split into an accompaniment of continuous quavers; **(d)** the piece is in a major key, with no modulations or chromatic notes; **(e)** balanced (periodic) phrasing, simple (functional) harmonies, melody-dominated texture, use of cadential six-four at ends of phrases.

No. 6 **(a)** The texture at the end consists of block chords while at the start it is monophonic (single melodic line), other textures include two-part writing and (at the start of the third section) octaves; **(b)** modal; **(c)** they are all of the same length, each begins with a similar motif and each ends with three block chords; **(d)** the combination of shifting tonal centres, modality, irregular phrase lengths and sparse textures suggests 20th century.

No. 7 **(a)** It remains in the same minor key throughout (using all three forms of the minor scale); **(b)** in the first half there is a two-part texture in which the melody is accompanied by a walking bass part that includes a number of octave leaps, in the second half there is a three-part texture in which the bass moves in rapid scale patterns; **(c)** in the bass part, in the middle of the piece; **(d)** moderato, no; **(e)** baroque, suggested by continuous movement driving through cadence points and the largely contrapuntal texture.

No. 8 **(a)** Atonal (the music has no fixed key centre); **(b)** the harmonic interval of a major 3rd, used as a type of ostinato; **(c)** there is a contrast between very short, isolated staccato notes and a few brief legato passages; **(d)** the tempo slows a little just after the middle, returns to it original slow speed, and agaom slows a little at the end; **(e)** the angular melodic writing, occasional extreme dissonance and atonal style all suggest 20th century.

No. 9 **(a)** They all start with the same dotted rhythm; **(b)** chordal; **(c)** major key with a number of chromatic harmonies (there are no real modulations); **(d)** see score; **(e)** the chromatic harmony, melody-dominated texture and frequent changes in dynamics all suggest the romantic period.

No. 10 **(a)** The first and second phrases are similar (but have different endings), the third phrase provides more of a contrast, and the last phrase is similar to the second, but is extended by two bars (AA^{1}BA^2); **(b)** melody with chordal accompaniment (broken chords at the start of the third phrase); **(c)** major key throughout (with a dominant pedal in the inner part of the first two phrases and just one chromatic note at the end of the third phrase); **(d)** the melody-dominated texture, with lilting rhythm and eleganty balanced phrases; **(e)** the periodic phrasing, with alternating imperfect and perfect cadences, melody-dominated texture and functional harmonies.

No. 11 (a) The piece is in a minor key, but the frequent use of the flattened 7th (which often clashes with the raised 7th to create 'false relations') gives the music a modal feel and the piece ends with a 'tierce de Picardie' (a major tonic chord at the end of a passage in a minor key; **(b)** contrapuntal (or polyphonic), although with only limited use of imitation; **(c)** there is no dynamic variety; **(d)** the lingering modality, false relations, tierce de picardie and texture of free counterpoint (with only short points of imitation) suggest the renaissance.

No. 12 (a) Monophonic at the start (a single bass line), after which the texture consists of two melodic parts (often in 3rds) above a walking bass; **(b)** it repeats the same pattern throughout the piece (an ostinato) – like many ground basses, it changes pitch (to the subdominant, for two repetitions) to provide variety in the middle of the piece; **(c)** it forms an introduction to the main part of the music; **(d)** there is a sudden change to forte for the middle section and another sudden change to piano for the last section ('terraced dynamics'); **(e)** it is in a minor key, with a modulation (to the subdominant) for the middle section (there is also a 'false relation' shortly before the end); **(f)** all of the above points suggest that this is a ground bass piece from the baroque period.

Music engraving and typesetting by Musonix